ALL KINDS OF WRITING

Fun, practical activities:
stories, poetry, instructions
and even excuses

Richard Dawson

A Piccolo Original
Piccolo Books

Note to parents

The importance of writing

● Writing is a skill that has developed over thousands of years. People haven't always used writing to record or communicate language. Ancient civilizations and some cultures today rely on the spoken word and 'oracles' to record laws, cultural tradition and history. We now have a variety of machines to help record and communicate language: telephones, tape recorders, word processors and so on.
● Nevertheless, whatever the media, we still need to develop and practise using or 'creating' language: building up understanding of words and phrases, choosing the right words and phrases for the right situation, and so on, just as ancient storytellers would have developed and practised their storytelling skills.

Helping your child with creative writing

● It is important to realize that writing comes from *within* the child and this makes it easier than reading. Reading comes from outside, so that someone else's ideas and clues have to be processed. The most important thing in writing is having something to say.
● A child cannot think of a word or phrase and understand its meaning and use unless he has heard it before, so in order to be able to write creatively, children first need to have as wide an experience of language as possible. They can gain this through stories, tapes, talk in the family, television, outings and so on.
● It is extremely difficult for anyone, even a professional writer, to create a perfect piece of work first time. So give your child plenty of help and understanding when writing – and above all, PRAISE.
● At first, concentrate on *content* and don't pay too much attention to spelling, grammar, punctuation, crossings out and so on.
● Talk about the subject before starting but try to encourage your child's thinking rather than giving your own suggestions. Give help with words where necessary, but together build on your child's ideas and expressions. Talk about the final result, what the words mean, what the child is trying to say, whether there are other ways of saying it – but always in a positive way.
● As your child's confidence grows, decide sometimes to do a draft first and then go on to a polished version, paying more attention to presentation. Don't do this every time; re-copying can become a chore and very off-putting.
● You could start a 'writing busy book' to develop extra ideas or record other writing you think is good or enjoyable.
● Encourage your child to judge his *own* work and to take pride in good presentation as well as good content. To help judge success in communicating and presentation, this book has a simple system of evaluation after some of the exercises.
● If your child has difficulty with fluent handwriting, you may sometimes like to help write out a piece in his own words. (See also helpful exercises in *Practise Together: Handwriting 2.*)
● Don't spend too long working on this book if you think your child's attention is wandering. It is important to do the activities in short bursts; when they stop being fun, it is time for a rest and a change.

The exercises in this book

● Each exercise in this book is designed to develop a form of expression: writing dialogue, persuading, describing, giving excuses and so on. In each case, the skill practised is indicated at the top of the page.
● The exercises are arranged in a particular order, so that the child can build up the skills and gain confidence in writing as they work through the book.
● They include examples of a wide variety of writing types: adverts, instructions, word pictures, as well as poetry and stories.

Factual Writing

My name is

first names . . . .

nickname . . . .

family name . . . .

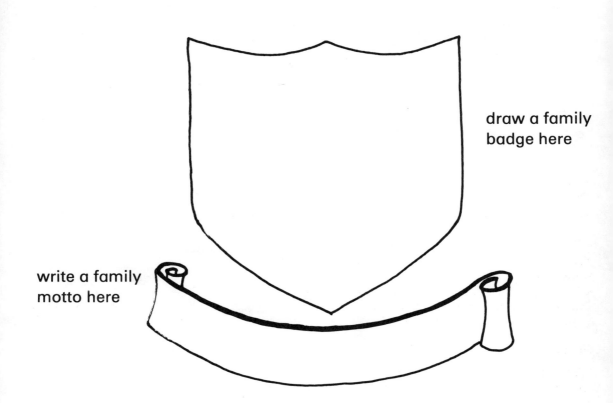

draw a family badge here

write a family motto here

Story Writing

Have you ever been camping? Did it go as planned? If you follow the footprints you could write this camping story.

Why not tell the story to someone before you start writing?

These words may help you.

bull **tent** **jump** **hedge** **wasp's nest** **pond**

Which of these is the best title for the story?

The camping holiday ☐

The wasp's nest ☐

Beware of the bull ☐

or perhaps you can think of a better title?

Did you like this story? ☺ 😐 ☹

Ending a story

Look carefully at the set of pictures. Can you tell someone the story? You can colour in the pictures whilst you are thinking, if you like.

Can you finish the story here?

_____

_____

_____

_____

_____

_____

_____

_____

_____

_____

_____

_____

_____

_____

Did you like the story? ☺ ☻ ☹

Read it to someone else.
Did they like it? ☺ ☻ ☹

> **Listen carefully to the beginning of the story. Allow your child to tell the story in his own way but encourage interesting use of adjectives and expression.**

Beginning a story

If you look at the picture on the next page, you will see the ending of a story, called:

The very strange plant

Can you write the beginning of this story?

_____
_____
_____
_____
_____
_____
_____

Did you like the story? 😊 😐 ☹️

Read the story to someone else.
Did they like the story? 😊 😐 ☹️

Show the story to someone.
Did they think it looked neat? 😊 😐 ☹️

> **Talk about the story but try to encourage your child's thinking rather than giving your suggestions then, together, build on your child's ideas.**

9

Excuses/Dialogue

Do you ever need to give a good excuse?

What excuse did the girl give to her teacher?

_____
_____
_____
_____
_____
_____
_____
_____

Do you think her teacher believed her?
_____

Pretend you did.
Can you think of a good excuse?

_____
_____
_____
_____
_____
_____

What excuse is the man giving his wife for how he smashed in the front of their car?

_____
_____
_____
_____
_____

Discuss the possible words that one could use. Emphasize the use of words like 'please', etc.

Persuasion/Dialogue

Jack has climbed the beanstalk and just reached the giant's house.
He knocks on the door and the giant's wife opens it.
What does Jack say to the giant's wife to persuade her to let him in?

You want a new bike.
What would you say to your grandad to persuade him to buy you one?

You want to go out to see your friends instead of doing the washing up.
What could you say to get out of doing the job?

Accurate description

Colour in the dog pictures.
Pretend one of the dogs is yours but it's lost. Describe him to a policeman.

_____

_____

_____

_____

_____

_____

_____

_____

these words may help you:- collar,
large, small, hair, tail, ears, legs, nose
own, black, white, spotted, friendly, fierce

One of these men has just robbed a bank.
Colour them in.

Decide which one was the robber and describe him to a policeman.

_____

_____

_____

_____

_____

_____

_____

These words may help you:—
big fat tall skinny glasses
scruffy bald moustache curly
short jacket sweater tie

Reporting

What do you think happens next?

What has happened?

What do you think will happen next?

> **Stories are made up of beginnings, middles and endings, each of which is equally important for the story to succeed. This exercise is to help children think carefully about the endings of the stories which should be both appropriate to the overall story and interesting.**

Dialogue

The girl wants to go out on her new bike.
What do you think her dad is saying to her?

Can you write this conversation using speech marks instead of speech bubbles?

'
_____
_____
_____ ' asked the girl.
'
_____
_____
_____ ' replied her dad.

Now what is the girl saying to her dad?

Write out the conversation between the girl and her dad.

_____
_____
_____
_____
_____

Point out that only the words which are actually spoken go in the speech bubbles. These same words then go inside the speech marks "...".

19

Rhyme/Poetry

Read this poem:

Gliding down the staircase,
Slipping through the door,
Not a sound, no footsteps
Clattering on the floor.

Can I hear a clicking?
No, a buzzing sound?
Could it be the noise of chains
Clanking on the ground?

Now a weird moaning,
And a fearful G-R-O-A-N!
Is it a GHOST or SPECTRE? No!
Just my sister on the phone!

Did you think the beginning of this poem sounded spooky?

20

Do you think you could write a spooky poem?
Write down all the 'ghosty' words you can think of.

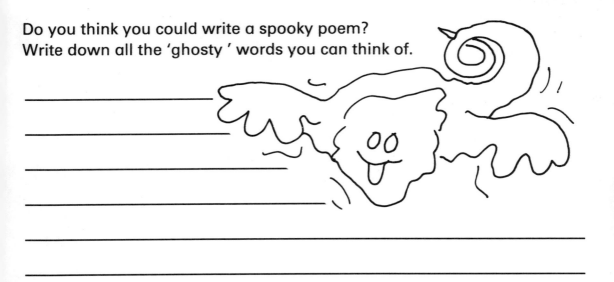

_____
_____
_____
_____

_____
_____

Here is the first verse of a poem.
Look at the words you have written down and use them to write the second verse.

Creak on the floor,
Bang on the stair,
Rattle on the door,
Straightening of hair!

You could write more verses and make a poem with plenty of spooky atmosphere!

| Word pictures |

You can use words to make pictures.

Can you make some word pictures using these words?

juggling   wobbling   shrinking   growing

Word pictures are called concrete poems.
Here is a fruity one!

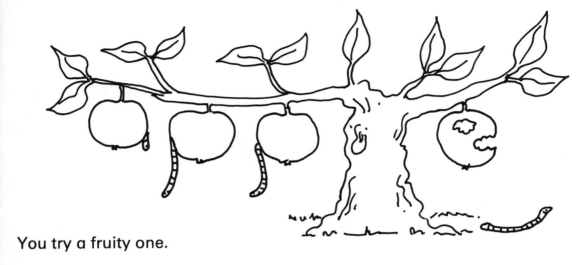

You try a fruity one.

Here is a more complicated one.

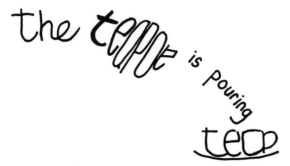

Can you write another one here?

Persuading/Advertising

When advertising a product, it is often best to use only a few words.

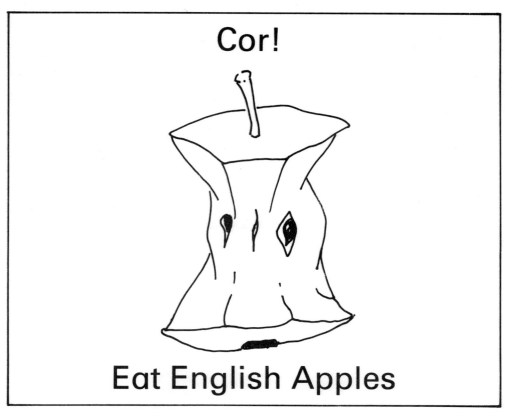

Cor!

Eat English Apples

Can you think of a slogan persuading people to eat more eggs?

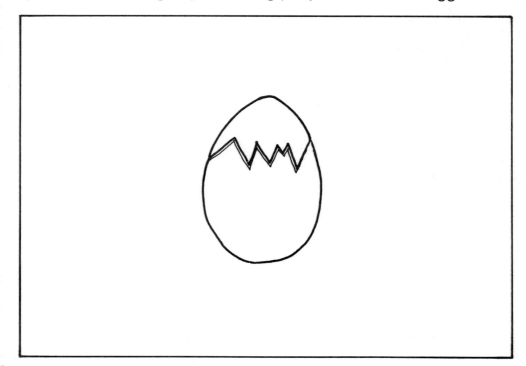

Can you design a milk advertisement with a catchy slogan?

Talk about how adverts are eye-catching, often humorous and easy to remember. Go through some magazines with your children and look at the different adverts.

Instructions

Can you write instructions for making a cup of tea?

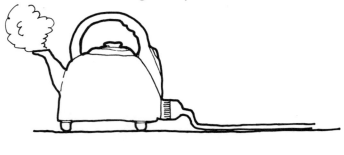

___
___
___

___
___
___

___
___
___

With a grown-up, follow your instructions and make a cup of tea.
Did they work? 😊 😐 🙁

> **Instructions require concise but accurate writing. Talk through the instructions. Let your child write them, then follow them together and make a cup of tea. Try a simple recipe as well.**

Description of incident

Look at the pictures and write the beginning of the story.

Draw what happens next . . .

. . . and finish the story.

Did you enjoy your story? 🙂 😐 🙁

Use the first two pictures to plan the story. There are lots of clues to help. Drawing the picture will help develop the plot. Read it back and judge the enjoyment value together.

Reporting personal emotions

Lost

Write the story.

Talk about being lost and how you would feel. If possible , get the child to recall
the times he has been lost and how he felt then.

Letter writing

Would you like to write a letter to the publishers of this book, telling them why you enjoyed, or maybe didn't enjoy, doing the activities?

Write your letter on this page.

Practise Together Editor
Piccolo Books
Cavaye Place
London SW10 9PG

Help the child to lay out the letter with the address, date and Dear ... in the right place. Suggest an appropriate ending.